First published in the
United States of America in 1997
by UNIVERSE PUBLISHING
A Division of
Rizzoli International Publications, Inc.
300 Park Avenue South
New York, NY 10010

Design: Daniel Petrucelli

Produced by CD Productions, NYC

97 98 99 / 10 9 8 7 6 5 4 3 2 1

Printed in England by Butler & Tanner Ltd,
Frome and London

Preceding page: Dominique Dawes
This page: Jordan Jovtchev
Facing page: John Macready

GYMNASTICS
BALANCING ACTS

CHRISTINA LESSA

Introduction by Bela Karolyi
Forewords by Shannon Miller and Dominique Dawes

UNIVERSE

preface

The first time I ventured into the realm of gymnastics was at the YMCA. I was ten years old and had just convinced my mother that ballet was not my thing. It didn't take much convincing since my lack of talent was obvious. When I started gymnastics class, my driving force was the vision I held of Nadia Comaneci performing at Madison Square Garden. After about a week of classes, I arrived at the decision that I was ready to try an Olympic-level dismount off the balance beam. I fractured my wrist and quickly resumed the role of admiring spectator.

From that point on, anyone who could move in ways that I could not instantly became my hero. My older sister was captain of her cheerleading squad, and I tirelessly sat through her tumbling practices on the front lawn. I also remember being captivated by my mother's yoga routine and her daily headstands. My uncle, a former ballet dancer, although diagnosed with multiple sclerosis and forbidden to exert himself, would secretly entertain me at family functions with pirouette after pirouette.

Unfortunately, I never realized my dream of athletic prowess, so it became my quest to

capture magical moments on film and share them with others. Over the course of this project, I was able to photograph and interview some of the most accomplished gymnasts of this century. It is impossible to describe what it's like to be five feet away from an athlete like Jaycie Phelps while she performs ariel after back-flip after ariel on a beam of wood no wider than your hand.

I found that all of the gymnasts share the same high standard of commitment, but that each athlete has as unique a story as they do a style. Without their exuberance and tremendous professionalism, this project would have been impossible. Not only did they give their best gymnastics performances, but their willingness and bravery to help make my visions a reality went beyond my expectations. Shannon Miller, for example, balanced barefoot on top of a horse in the middle of a February snowstorm; Dominique Dawes posed fearlessly on the roof edge of a skyscraper above Times Square; Trent Dimas soared through the air above a steep incline (with no crash pad) in front of the Statue of Liberty...

This book is a tribute to the gymnasts, and to the hope they inspire in all of us.

—Christina Lessa, New York City, May, 1997

INTRODUCTION by BELA KAROLYI

In the beginning I WAS UNCERTAIN HOW TO CHOOSE MY FATE: should I become A DOCTOR, A LAWYER, A FARMER — *OR WHAT?*

My mother once handed me an appliance and asked me to fix it. I boldly took it in hand and attempted to make it work. After a short time it exploded in my hands, and I knew then that I was not to be an engineer. Gymnastics offered a solution to my problem.

When I was in college, I was obligated to participate in Systematic Gymnastic Preparation in order to pass my mandatory student test at the Physical Education University in Bucharest. The experience, which started out as one of the worst I'd ever had, became the deepest passion of my life.

I struggled through the difficulties of catching up in this sport that was completely new to me. I realized that gymnastics was the purest physical and mental challenge of all sports I had tried. After recognizing this reality, I discovered more exciting and unique aspects of this beautiful sport. It gave me the extraordinary opportunity to communicate with my audience by combining the ele-ments of music and art into an expressive performance from my heart. Even though I never achieved remarkable athletic success in gymnastics, I fell deeply in love with it and chose to turn it into my lifelong profession and vocation.

Gymnastics is not for the faint of heart, nor for the heartless. It requires a perfect balance of physical and mental strength and flexibility. I have always admired and been amazed by the level of dedication, love, and most important, the incredible ability of the hundreds of young girls I have had the honor to work with and coach towards excellence. In addition to helping them achieve athletic fame, I receive great satisfaction knowing that gymnastics has given the girls self-confidence, competitiveness, discipline, the ability to set goals, a desire to strive for excellence, and an understanding of love. There is nothing in the world I would trade for the unforgettable memories provided by this sublime sport and its participants, the gymnasts.

I have also been fortunate enough to enjoy the sincere friendship of many great men, some coaches and gymnasts, through whom I have shared the world of men's gymnastics. The men who compete in this sport are also deserving of praise for their integrity, talent, and, yes, sensitivity.

Gymnastics: Balancing Acts showcases the most exceptional representatives of this ultimate activity; which is more than a sport, more than art, and more than what seems possible to describe with ordinary words. These representatives are role models who inspire millions of people, young and old, inviting them to be a part of the magical world of gymnastics.

In a unique way, this book focuses both on the athletic ability and artistic talents of these tremendous athletes. They are represented not as robots or athletic machines, but in a way that gives us an insight into their personalities and into their hearts. The public has seen the emotional intensity during competition, victories, and defeats, and on the podium when medals are won or lost—but no one, until now, has managed to bring out such an individually tailored, true portrait of these fine people as performers. Each portrait is a window into the spirit of the gymnast.

It is an important record for them and for those who love them; not just the single moment when a miracle changed their life, but the miracle of what lives inside each of them. It is also a tribute to the artistic elements of this great sport and what it is that makes the whole world love gymnastics. Through this book, everyone can appreciate the most important aspect of gymnastics: the human desire to communicate to others—through finely honed and energy-filled, impossible movements—something very personal and private that every observer can feel and understand.

Bela Karolyi, Texas, 1997

7

Foreword by
SHANNON MILLER

JUST BEFORE MY FIFTH BIRTHDAY, MY MOM SUGGESTED TO MY OLDER SISTER, TESSA, AND ME THAT MAYBE WE SHOULD THINK ABOUT TAKING GYMNASTICS CLASSES. Santa had brought us a trampoline for Christmas just a few months earlier, and my parents watched Tessa and me doing flips on it and jumping all over the place — they were beginning to get worried. Tessa and I had decided we were bored with dance, so Mom and Dad thought maybe they could channel our energies into gymnastics...at least for a while. It sounded like fun so we agreed to take some lessons. We both loved tumbling, doing somersaults, running and jumping, and even walking on the beam. That July 4th, the coach at the gym was asked if some of the students would march in the Edmond parade. After we got started, I noticed some of the older girls doing back walkovers and other skills. I wanted to show off a little too but I hadn't totally mastered a back walkover. My mom had to run along on the side of the street and each time I was ready to perform, she would dash out and make sure I didn't land on my head as I bent backwards.

I have now been in gymnastics for over fifteen years and I've never loved this sport more. It has so much to offer both on the floor and off. Gymnastics is not only a fantastic sport in itself, but is an excellent preparation for other sports. You must develop strength, flexibility, and physical endurance, while exhibiting poise and grace under pressure. When competing, you had better be prepared to literally think on your feet (or head, as the case may be.) I learned to be disciplined and organized in order to balance gymnastics training, school, and a social and family life. You don't have to win a medal in gymnastics to feel great. Learning a new skill, improving routines, handling fear, all help you feel good about yourself. These are the rewards that keep me going.

Most people think of gymnastics as an individual sport, but it is really much more of a team sport than people realize. Every day in the gym we pull boards for each other, help set bars, loan each other tape, shoes, and grips, help each other condition, share secrets and helpful hints, laugh and cry together. We form friendships that last long after our competitive days. In the 1996 Olympics, we discovered the supreme high of setting aside our individual desires to achieve a common goal. Supporting each other and feeling true joy for each member's accomplishments was a magical experience I will carry in my heart for the rest of my life.

In addition to all that gymnastics teaches, it can bring so much pleasure. I've traveled to numerous places, and have seen sights most people only read about; I've met athletes from all over the world, and have experienced many different cultures; I've had the joy of seeing the eager smiles on the faces of children at clinics I've taught, and the pleasure of holding a small child at a hospital as I helped raise money for the Children's Miracle Network. Gymnastics has given me so much, and has provided me with the means to give back to my community.

To all those youngsters thinking of pursuing gymnastics, I would like to say: dare to dream, but be prepared to follow those dreams with hard work, dedication, and persistence. There are only seven spots on the Olympic gymnastics team, but there's all the room in the world to have fun and improve yourself physically and mentally. Never limit yourself, but do set some smaller, more immediate goals. These will help you work steadily towards your long-term goal, and let you know you are making progress. A fan once sent me a quote from football coach, Paul "Bear" Bryant, that sums up my philosophy pretty well: "If you believe in yourself and have dedication and pride, never quit and you'll be a winner. The price of victory is high, but so are the rewards."

— Shannon Miller, Edmond, OK, 1997

WHEN YOU SEE GYMNASTICS ON TV IT LOOKS FLAWLESS, BUT UNDERNEATH YOU HAVE TO DEAL WITH A LOT OF PRESSURES: THE MENTAL AND PHYSICAL DISCIPLINE AS WELL AS POLITICS AND FEAR.

When you watch a competitor in an event, what you see is only the tip of the iceberg compared to all of the preparation that goes into getting the person to that point. When I received my gold and bronze medals I wasn't only receiving them for myself, but for a whole team of people: my family, my coach, my psychologist, my schoolteachers, my physicians, my teammates, and my friends. They all deserve a piece of those medals, too.

In gymnastics you have to face your fears every day. It might be your fear of getting hurt by attempting a new skill, or your fear of competing and not doing your best. I am always concerned about how well I'm doing, but not to impress anyone else or just to please my coach; ever since I was young, it has just been gymnastics and me, and I care about being the best I can be for me.

My coach, Kelli Hill, always stressed the importance of education, and she's right. The goal of getting into college is just as important as the goal of getting into the Olympics. I think you can learn a lot, whatever you do, as long as you have the right attitude. I have always been attracted to hard work — that's part of what made me love gymnastics so much.

Gymnastics is a tough sport, but its rewards are huge. I think everyone should try gymnastics — not so they can be world champions, but so they can learn more about themselves as people and discover what their strengths and weaknesses are.

When I was little I wanted to be an undercover FBI agent because I liked the idea of

playing different roles. I also used to pick my favorite character from a TV show and act out their part for my mom. I have always loved acting and showing off different sides of my personality. In gymnastics, it is your personality that makes you or breaks you in the eyes of your fans.

The recognition I've gained from gymnastics has helped me pursue my second ambition, acting.

Balancing Acts is the first book I've done where I'm not just Dominique Dawes, the gymnast who won a medal, but Dominique Dawes, the person who loves to act and have fun.

-— Dominique Dawes, NYC, 1997

Foreword by
DOMINIQUE
DAWES

SHANNON MILLER

I never cared about becoming famous. That was never my goal. When

I finally got around to thinking I might be able to make an Olympic

team, the implication was not that the accomplishment might boost

me to stardom, rather that I would have proved something to myself—

that all the long hours, sacrifice, hard work, and dedication to

my sport would allow me the opportunity to represent my country

at the highest level. Others would respect me for my achievement,

and I would respect myself. It truly was an awesomely inspiring

experience to march out onto the competition floor wearing the

U.S. warm-up and knowing all of America was rooting for me to

do my very best. There is just no other feeling like that.

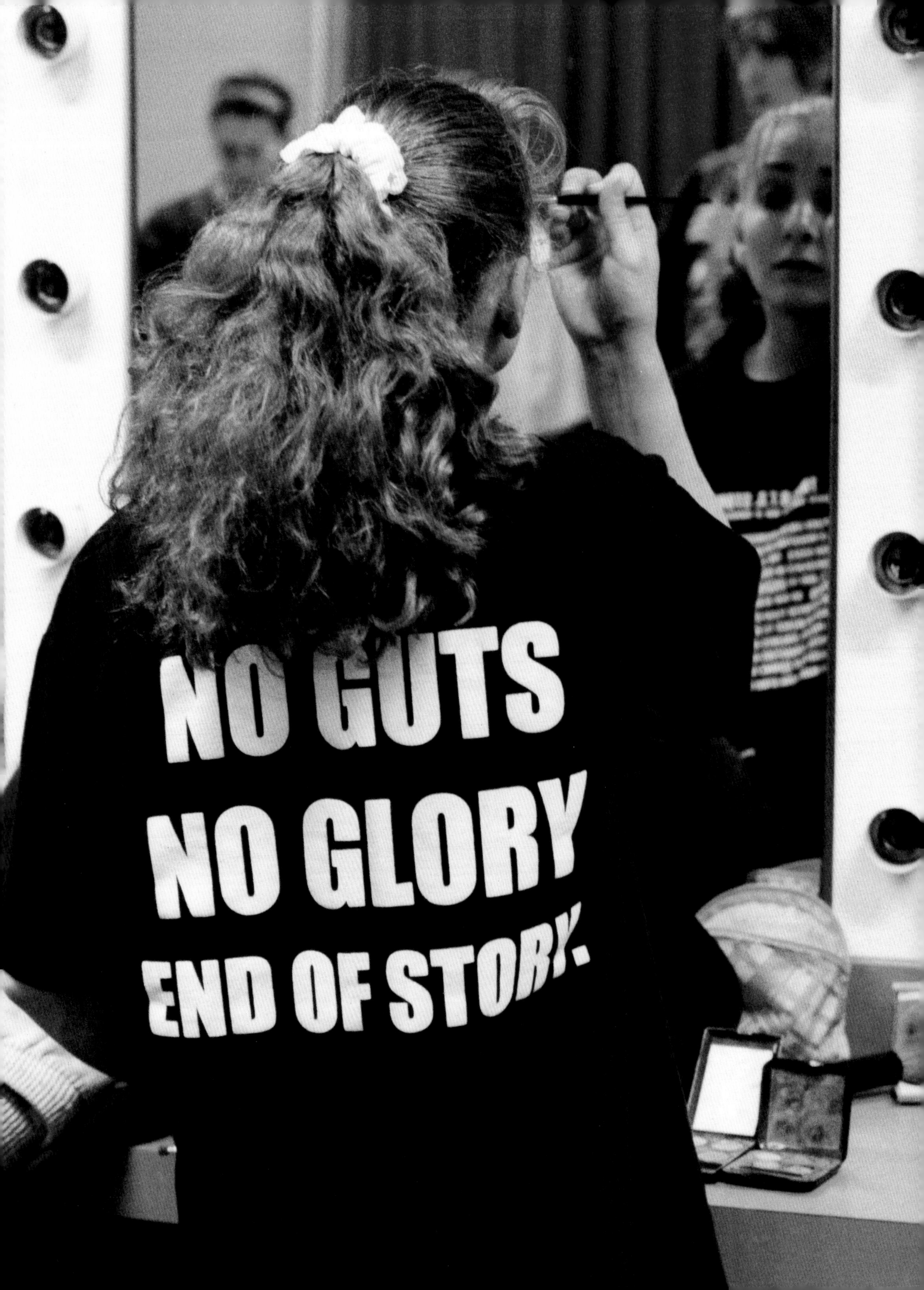
NO GUTS
NO GLORY
END OF STORY.

We are all role models whether we choose to be or not. Someone old or young is always watching and possibly being influenced by our behavior. I try my best to set a good example.

I can't imagine what I would change about my career. I was able to train with two of the best gymnastics coaches in the sport, live at home with my family, go to public school with the kids I grew up with, graduate with my class, travel to all parts of the world and still have time to take annual family vacations, help decorate and cook at Christmas, watch my favorite TV shows, visit the mall, take in a movie or a hockey game now and then, get advice from my older sister, give advice to my younger brother — what more could I ask for? Whether they aspire to compete, or just want to experience the thrill of improving their strength, flexibility, and grace, I hope I have been able to show young girls in the U.S., and maybe all over the world, that gymnastics is a beautiful and enjoyable sport. Hopefully, the successes I have enjoyed prove that with hard work, determination, patience, and faith you can accomplish almost anything. I hope that my perseverance in gymnastics, in spite

LIVING A SIMPLE LIFE IS A DREAM COME TRUE

of all of the dim predictions that I was getting too old to compete successfully, has demonstrated to people that this is no longer a sport just for young girls — but also a sport for women. So, I hope I have shown adults and children alike that if you take a fall, literally or figuratively, you can pick yourself up, trust in God's care, and achieve your dreams.

Shannon and Maharajah, Robin's Nest Farm, New Jersey

DOMINIQUE
DAWES

I have been a gymnast for fourteen years, and every year has had its ups and downs. There have been times in my career when I felt as though I had to prove my ability more than other gymnasts because of my race. I've had to fight to earn my place in the spotlight.

One of my current ambitions is to help open the sport to all minorities. Early in my career, I didn't realize just how few black people there are in gymnastics. My coach, Kelli Hill, and I, being of different backgrounds, have worked together very successfully. She's my greatest supporter and has been like family to me. I believe that we have shown that differences in race are not negative factors unless you choose to see them in that light.

EXTREME MOT

ION

I believe in living life to the fullest — we don't know when our time is up. I have always had an excessive amount of energy. I was walking by the age of eight months, and my family knew that I would always be on the go. But no one could have predicted that movement would dominate my future. I have learned that before you set your mind to anything in life, you must first learn to love and to respect yourself.

Only YOU can define your own failures and successes. I am blessed to have accomplished so much in the gymnastics arena. Up until now, my life has been filled with so many wonderful moments, but I know the BEST moments are yet to come.

PETER VIDMAR

In gymnastics and in life, if you take the risk to be yourself, you will earn the most respect.

When my father was 29, he was diagnosed with polio. He wasn't

able to be athletic himself, so he encouraged me to try to reach

my physical potential and to move in ways that he could not. My

gymnastics career began at age eleven, when my parents answered

a newspaper ad placed by renowned coach Makodo Sakamodo that

simply read, "Future Olympic Champions Sought." I joined the gym

because I wanted to have fun, but Sakamodo was serious about his

offer. By age thirteen, I was daydreaming about gymnastics all

the time. I learned early that to become a champion you have to

have the guts to imagine yourself as better than the best guy around.

GYMNASTS ARE HIGH-RISK ADDICTS AND EXTREME THRILL SEEKERS

I consider gymnastics to be the fastest-moving sport on the entire planet. We all want to outdo one another. The master of risk-taking was my Olympic teammate Mitch Gaylord. He had an uncanny knack for achieving the impossible, like the trick "the Gaylord flip" from the 1984 Games. In 1996 no one even attempted it. Still, the level of difficulty is climbing at a very rapid pace — we're always discovering just how far we can push the envelope.

I believe **we are all given gifts.** It is our duty to use them to the best of our ability. I always felt that **if I achieved success,** I would acknowledge God's hand in all things.

I was so quiet when I was young. My mother wanted to

start me in ballet so I'd become more outgoing, but I

wasn't old enough, so she enrolled me in gymnastics

instead. When I was five, and old enough for ballet, I

didn't want to leave the gym. I had fallen in love

with gymnastics — it broke me out of my shell.

AMY CHOW

I was bouncing around everywhere. Why just walk across

a room? I somersaulted, cartwheeled, or walked on my hands.

I even broke my toe on the corner of the desk doing a

roundoff in my room. Gymnastics made me feel unique — I

liked being able to do things that most people coudn't.

Gymnastics to me is the challenge of learning new skills and the pride it brings when you master them. At the 1994 World Championships in Germany, I completed a brand new skill on uneven bars that would later be named after me. It was a Stalder with one and one-half pirouettes. For me, what's even more exciting than winning medals is that a drawing and description of my move, the "CHOW," will forever be printed on the judges' Code of Points.

ACCOMPLISHMENT
DOESN'T
ELIMINATE FEAR.

— IVAN

SOMETIMES YOU
HAVE TO TRUST
SOMEONE ELSE
more than
YOU TRUST
YOUR-
SELF.

— JORDAN

After trying and failing
all day,

INSPIRATION

exhausted and ready
to give up,
one of us achieves
the impossible.

LILIA PODKOPAYEVA

I was born in a very poor region of eastern Ukraine, called Donetsk, on August 15, 1978. I lived in a one-room flat with my mother, grandmother, grandfather, brother, and my father. My parents divorced when I was two.

At the age of five I began my gymnastics career. Grandma would travel with me by train six days a week. Because she put so much effort into my career, I was inspired to take it all very seriously. My greatest strength I inherited from her: an iron will and an ability to concentrate. I won my first competition at the age of six. By the time I was ten, my dream was to become champion of my small town, by fourteen the Ukraine, and by eighteen the world.

Galina Losinskaya has been my coach for thirteen years. She is my second mother—I have spent more time with her than anyone else. She taught me about gymnastics and about life. She helps me with my schooling and stays by me when I am ill. I appreciate all that she has done—she left her own family for me.

On my way to the 1996 Olympics, my grandmother died. I was very upset, but I knew she would want me to compete. So with Galina's support, I fulfilled our dream. I won the all-around Olympic gold, and became the first woman to become World, European, and Olympic champion all in the same year. In this one competition, I attained everything we had all worked for. I dedicated it to my grandmother. I know she was there with me.

GYMNASTICS IS NOT JUST ABOUT JUMPING AROUND, BUT IS AN ENTIRE LIFESTYLE.

I RESPECT GYMNASTS LIKE SCHERBO AND BOGINSKAYA BECAUSE THEY PERFORM AND

COMPETE LIKE PROFESSIONALS. GYMNASTICS IS ALSO AN OBSESSION. I LOVE IT

AND CAN'T LIVE WITHOUT IT. WHEN I DON'T HAVE TO TRAIN ON SUNDAYS

I FEEL TERRIBLE AND I HAVE TO DO SOMETHING WHERE I CAN

MOVE MY BODY. IT'S SO MUCH MORE

INTERESTING THAN JUST

LYING AROUND WATCHING TV.

When I'm in front of an
audience, I see nothing
around me — I just
perform.

But still I
know everyone
is watching. When
I'm performing for
the crowd, I feel
responsible to give my
very best. I used to
watch the ballet and old
movies. This taught me to
express myself and let my
feelings shine through each
character.

JAIR LYNCH

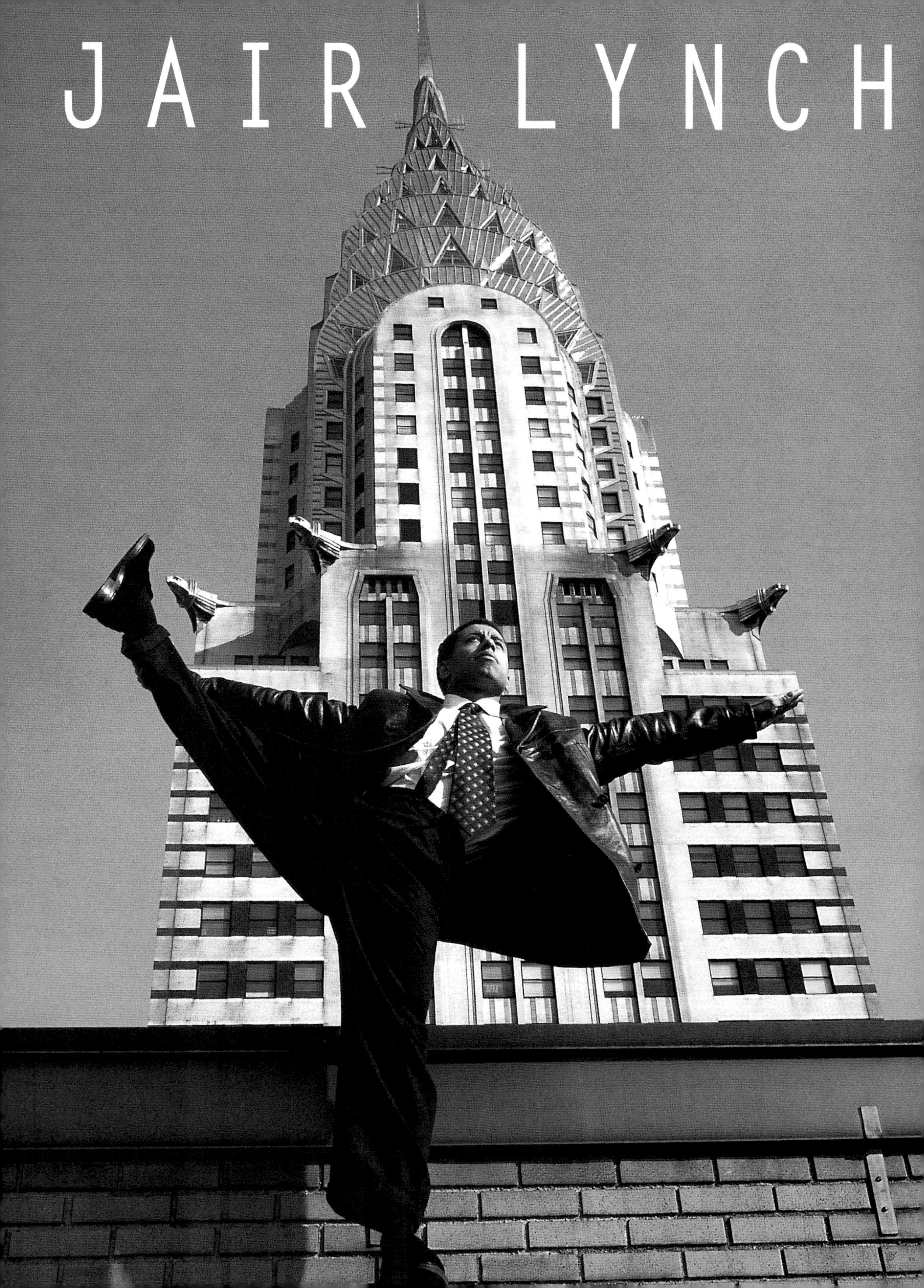

AS THE SECOND BLACK GYMNAST TO COMPETE AT AN OLYMPIC GAMES AND THE FIRST TO WIN A MEDAL — HOW DOES IT FEEL TO BE CONSIDERED A HERO?

IS THERE ANYTHING IN YOUR LIFE THAT COULD EVER TAKE THE PLACE OF GYMNASTICS?

I have been in the gym for 16 of my 25 years. Gymnastics has provided structure for my life, and in that way has given me a certain amount of control over what I do and accomplish. Now that I'm retired, I need to readjust my life to fill that void. I have two degrees from Stanford in design and engineering and I'm thinking of applying them to real estate or architecture. These careers interest me because they are all about creating structures and watching their development. As in gymnastics, I want to leave my mark.

For my fans to consider me a hero is a great honor, but I am really just an extension of tremendous athletes like Jesse Owens, Arthur Ashe, and Jackie Robinson, who have paved the way for me and broken down the color barriers. I need to carry the torch for the next generation.

My goal is to provide opportunities for minority kids to get involved in sports like gymnastics, which traditionally are not as open to minorities. I'd like them to be able to experience what I've learned. People like myself, Dominique Dawes, and Amy Chow reflect the racial diversity of this country within the sport of gymnastics. We've come a long way, but there's still so much more that needs to be done.

IF GYMNASTICS PROVIDED THE STRUCTURE IN YOUR LIFE, WHERE DID YOU FIND THE SUPPORT?

In gymnastics, you have to sacrifice a lot of your free time that you would normally spend at home. It's the support and understanding from your family and friends that gets you through. It's a personal balancing act that allows you to live your life and still perform at your best. My parents had a strong commitment to my dreams that I am thankful for every day. Who was paying the bills? Who was driving me to the gym? Who was handling the broken bones? Who had to think beyond what the traditional parental commitments were...they went beyond all of this and I adore them for it.

IF I HAD been named JOE, I might have SEEN MYSELF as THE AVERAGE JOE. I MIGHT NOT HAVE TRIED AS HARD TO EXCEL!

JAIR
(jy-ear')
means "one who sees the light"
IN SENEGALESE

My most rewarding

moment was stepping onto

the platform for a parallel

bar finals with my hands

bloodied. A ripped callous

had become such a hindrance

that I had to slice away

the skin from my hand with a razorblade

just moments before I started my routine

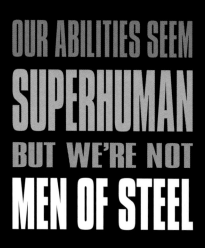

OUR ABILITIES SEEM SUPERHUMAN BUT WE'RE NOT MEN OF STEEL

and had to push myself beyond

the pain and focus on control.

I was so focused that I got

into a "zone" — that state of

mind athletes talk about, where

you feel in full control and

know that you can perform at your

absolute highest level no matter what

MARK HENRY, OLYMPIC WEIGHTLIFTER,
IS A VERY GOOD FRIEND OF MINE.
WE TRAINED TOGETHER AT THE
OLYMPIC TRAINING CENTER DURING
COMPETITION.

HE CARRIED ME
THROUGH THE INTENSITY
OF EATING, DRINKING, AND SLEEPING GYMNASTICS.

OUR RELATIONSHIP IS
STRONG
BECAUSE OF A MUTUAL RESPECT

FOR WHAT THE OTHER HAS BEEN

THROUGH.

WE SHARED THE COMMITMENT AND

SACRIFICE IT TAKES TO TRY TO BE

THE VERY BEST.

dominique
moceanu

I was nine when I started train-ing at Bela's camp. I was placed in a group with gymnastics stars like Kim Zmeskal and Betty Okino. I was the youngest. When Bela started to train the older girls for the Olympics, I was put back into a group with kids my own age. That made me work harder, and all the time I thought, "I must become a great person...I want to become an Olympian."

A year later, when Bela came back for me, I was still the youngest, but I was ready. I won the 1995 National Competition and made the Olympic team.

As I have said many times, "I will always be grateful to all the people who helped me along the way, including my teammates, who have always been so supportive. I will always remember who I am, where I have come from, and how hard I have worked to get this far.

Sometimes I look in the mirror and pretend I am Dominique Moceanu the Olympic champion. And then I look in the mirror and see my regular feature, and that's good enough for me."

a blur

"Someone walking into an arena to witness a gymnastics meet for the very first time might have a pretty confused first impression. Unless you know what you're looking for, it probably appears to be

# of leotards flying through the air, surrounded by chalk dust.

Soon enough, though, you realize that gymnastics is the opposite of chaos."

FROM *Dominique Moceanu, An American Champion: An Autobiography*

gymnastics is
JUST ON THE EDGE
OF BEING
out of CONTROL.
Nothing's more fun than FLIPPING and TUMBLING...

Sometimes
I feel like
I just
CAN'T

STOP!

BART
CONNER

They say that gymnastics is 90% mental. How do you get focused?

By setting a high goal and admitting that it is important to you. This makes you vulnerable because you risk failing. It takes great courage.

HOW DID YOU SET YOURSELF APART?

I was never the most talented, but I have always been willing to work hard. I usually performed routines with adequate difficulty but no unnecessary risk. I tried to be stylish and present my routines with elegance, like the great Japanese champions Kasamotsu and Kato.

Rules to live by:

1. Dedication.

2. Set Goals.

3. Attention to Detail.

4. Handle Adversity.

5. Commitment.

6. Use the qualities developed in gymnastics in other areas.

Do you think you missed out on anything?

Some people think gymnasts miss out on a normal life. Most of us excel, however, because we want more than the normal. We all make *choices*, not sacrifices. If I have missed something, it probably wasn't that important anyway.

I love

It's my

the gym.

high-tech playground.

After 29

years,

it's

still

the place

where I

have the

most fun.

NADIA COMANECI

I AM A QUIET PERSON AND I HAVE A DIFFICULT TIME MAKING COMMENTS ABOUT

MYSELF. I AM GRATEFUL FOR THE OPPORTUNITIES I HAVE HAD AND I KNOW I WILL ALWAYS

BE REMEMBERED AS THE GYMNAST WHO SCORED THE PERFECT "10." BUT I GOT INVOLVED

IN GYMNASTICS ONLY BECAUSE I LOVED THE SPORT. I NEVER IMAGINED THAT IT

WOULD DEFINE MY LIFE. I DIDN'T KNOW VERY MUCH ABOUT THE OLYMPICS, AND HAD NO

IDEA I'D BECOME FAMOUS...I THOUGHT I WOULD GROW UP TO BECOME A SURGEON.

At the 1976 Olympics, while fourteen-year-old Nadia was causing a gymnastics revolution, eighteen-year-old Bart Conner was the youngest member of the U.S. men's Olympic gymnastics team. They had met each other for the first time in New York, a few months before the Olympics, at the awards ceremony for the American Cup Gymnastics Competition. Over the next thirteen years, they saw each other frequently at competitions. In 1989, Nadia defected from Romania with the help of a man named Constantin Panait. He led her and six others on foot through mud, snow, and ice until they reached freedom in Austria. Nadia left behind her family — she took with her only what she could carry. "It was very difficult leaving my family and friends behind, knowing that if the political system in Romania didn't change, I would never see them again."

Panait took Nadia to Florida and became her manager. It wasn't long, however, before Panait began to dominate her every move — controlling her and taking advantage of her celebrity status. Nadia was terrified of Panait, but felt helpless and unable to tell anyone about her situation. At this time, Bart saw Nadia on a television show and was concerned that she may be in trouble. He soon tracked her down and offered her help. Bart kept in contact with Nadia, and they became close friends over the phone. Soon after, they began to make appearances together and by the summer of 1991 they had fallen in love.

On November 12, 1994, Nadia's birthday, Bart proposed. They were married at a fairy-tale ceremony in Bucharest in April 1996 in front of 1,500 guests and a crowd of onlookers. "Being married to a successful athlete is wonderful," Nadia has said, "We complement each other and understand each other's experiences in the sport. We inspire people because we have found each other. Looking back, I wouldn't change anything at all about my life including the difficulties I lived through. Without my past I wouldn't be where I am today. It's been like a fairy tale..."

JOHN MACREADY

I think of gymnastics as a full-time job. I don't mean "job" in a
bad way — but it's definitely serious work. Every day I wake up
and go to the gym for seven to ten hours, and the reward for this
labor is the Olympics. For as long as I can remember, I have wanted to be an Olympian. To make it to the 1996 Olympics was the biggest
thrill of my life. Most of us weren't there to win a gold medal —
we were there to capture a team medal and to honor our country.

The most emotional moment was during the closing ceremonies.
I was able to sit as a spectator and watch with the enormous crowd of
people from all over the world. The size of the crowd absolutely
overwhelmed me. Then, Stevie Wonder came out and began singing John
Lennon's peace anthem, "Imagine." I started to cry, and when I looked
around me, I saw that everyone else was crying, too. It was then that
I realized what the Olympics — and sacrifice — are all about.

I think I SEE WOMEN DIFFERENTLY than most men because I see firsthand HOW STRONG WOMEN ARE. I CAN'T ACKNOWLEDGE the TYPICAL STEREOTYPES.

THE SEVEN GIRLS WHO MADE UP THE 1996 U.S. WOMEN'S GYMNASTICS TEAM HAVE PROVEN THAT WOMEN ARE JUST AS STRONG AS MEN AND CAN ACHIEVE ANYTHING THEY WANT — EVEN UNDER THE MOST DIFFICULT CIRCUMSTANCES. I CONSIDER MYSELF LUCKY TO KNOW SUCH INCREDIBLE WOMEN.

OLGA KORBUT

I was born into a simple Belarussian family in the small city of Grodno. We were considered very poor because my parents had to support four children and, at that time, it was a very heavy load to carry.

My parents had nothing to do with sports and never really cared what my sister and I did as long as we didn't bother them. We all turned out to be excellent athletes, two of us in gymnastics and two in volleyball. Although I was the only one who became world-famous, we all did very well for ourselves.

The most important moment of my life is probably the day when I was picked out by my future coach, Renald Knysh. He was very famous and it was nearly impossible to get onto his team. I was so frightened on that day and yet I felt that some superpower strength came over me. I did everything he asked and more...all of a sudden, I was doing moves that I had never done before and girls with two or three more years of extensive training would not have been able to do. After this, he chose me for the team, and placed me in the ten to eleven-year-old group. I was eight at the time. That day my life changed. It was the start of my gymnastics career.

When I think back, I have two treasured memories: The first was at the 1974 World Championships in Varna, when my coach said to me, "You will be a real champion when other athletes recognize you as a champion." That day, after my vault, every contestant applauded me. Normally, this never happens because everyone is concentrating on their own routine. To see all their attention on me was overwhelming. It was a moment that one can never, ever forget.

The second memory is of my first Olympics, in 1972. When I finished my routine on the uneven bars, the judges awarded me very low marks, only 9.7. I remember the whole arena protesting — yelling, screaming, and booing. They held up the Olympic Games for 25 minutes. It was unheard of. I felt extraordinarily sad and satisfied at the the same time — that's the sport, isn't it?

I OVERCAME TREMENDOUS HARDSHIP TO BECOME A GYMNAST— IT WAS MY FIRST LOVE

What do you consider to be some of the differences between American and Russian gymnastics? If you would have asked me that question several years ago, I would most certainly have answered that the Russian school is much better. But times changed, Russia fell apart and, as a result, lost its strength, while America made a huge leap forward. There is still, however, one thing that I feel is better about the Russian style of gymnastics — it is more feminine; the girls are more developed, more graceful, yet they can execute all the athletic elements that the smaller American girls can.

I SEE A LONG-NEEDED CHANGE COMING TO GYMNASTICS.

What do you see in the future of gymnastics? Gymnastics has generally remained the same since my time, except that it has become mainly acrobatic. Because of this, I think it is losing a certain audience. Before, people watched to see grace, beauty, poise, and at the same time, tremendous athletic ability. Now, I fear it's only to see the tricks. I think the new rule of limiting the starting competitive age to sixteen is wrong. I'm all for letting younger girls compete. There are so many girls who peak at twelve or thirteen years of age — they should not miss this moment of their lives. On the other hand, older gymnasts are struggling to survive. There is no way a woman in her twenties can compete with a fourteen-year-old on the same level, and they shouldn't have to. It's time for a change. It's time to separate gymnastics into two groups: up-to-fifteen, and sixteen-and-over. I feel that this change would prolong the life of gymnastics, force coaches to become more imaginative, and bring more participants and fans to the sport.

MY SUCCESS MARKED A MILESTONE IN
GYMNASTICS. I ONLY REALIZED LATER
IN MY LIFE WHAT AN IMPACT MY PER-
FORMANCE AT THE 1972 OLYMPICS HAD
ON YOUNG GIRLS ALL OVER THE WORLD.

"I AM PROUD TO BE A GROUNDBREAKER IN THE SPORT—
MY MISSION IS TO GIVE BACK
TO THE YOUNG
ALL THAT I HAVE LEARNED."

THAT YEAR, THEY SIGNED UP FOR GYM-
NASTICS CLASSES BY THE THOUSANDS.
NOW, THE NUMBERS ARE STAGGERING.

CHAINEY
UMPHREY

You gain incredible strength from gymnastics — both mental and physical. But you have

to be willing to go through its share of trials and sacrifices. On my first gymnastics

trip, in a restaurant with all my teammates, I was denied service because I was black.

I could have become disillusioned, but I felt even more motivated. I found that by

excelling and being in the public eye, I could help change these perceptions. I hope I've

shown that we all have the same hopes and desires, that we all want to succeed. In gym-

nastics you are also constantly pushing your physical limits. A number of times I've

gone too far. I broke a leg and two fingers but the worst was breaking and dislocating

my foot, which prevented me from competing in the 1992 Olympics. I didn't know if I would

ever walk again, and no one believed that I'd have the determi-

nation to continue competing. My sister, Frances, helped

me learn to walk again and regain my confidence so I could

go on to win a medal in the 1996 Olympics.

My injuries became a way to reaffirm my goals.

IN THE GYM WE ALL WANT THE SAME THING....

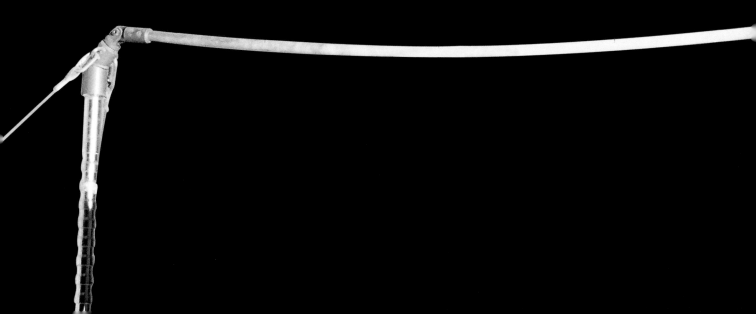

TO REACH THE
HEIGHT OF PERFECTION.

MARY LOU RETTON

I've always believed

that you can do

extraordinary things

if you rise above

your limits, both

real and imaginary.

"Taking risks and meeting challenges head-on can be dangerous to your COMFORT ZONE."

I never took the easy road on my way to success. I sought out new challenges and learned to recognize my strengths.

It wasn't long before my dream came true at the 1984 Olympics where I had the honor of winning five medals for my country.

FUN IS THE KEY WORD FOR ALL CHILDREN. I WAS NEVER FORCED

OR PUSHED INTO GYMNASTICS OR ANYTHING ELSE. I

WAS TAUGHT TO BELIEVE IN MYSELF AND MY ABILITIES AND I

WANT TO TEACH MY CHILDREN THE SAME. SELF-CONFIDENCE THROUGH

FUN, POSITIVE BEHAVIOR—THAT'S GYMNASTICS FOR ME.

KRASIMIR DUNEV

Was it always your dream to become a gymnastics champion?

I never thought about it when I was young. Actually, my dream was to be a movie star. Every time I saw the stars on the big screen I wanted to be just like them.

What is most memorable about your gymnastics career?

I am proud to be the first person ever to successfully execute SIX release combinations on the high bar, at the 1995 World Championships.

How do you feel about all the attention you've been getting in America?

In America, it seems people put a lot of emphasis on how a person looks. In Bulgaria, I was just average, no one said otherwise. The way I look is just a small part of who I am. I am most proud of my work and who I am becoming as a person.

I COMMITTED MY
WHOLE LIFE
TO WINNING A MEDAL
AT THE 1996
OLYMPICS.

IN ATLANTA
MY HIGH BAR WAS
NEARLY PERFECT.

MY EFFORTS PAID OFF.
COMMITMENT
IS MY MOTTO!

Krasimir Dunev, Santa Monica Pier

MITCH GAYLORD

I LOVED GYMNASTICS — I LOVED THE CALCULATED RISK. I WAS FEARLESS.

THIS BROUGHT ME A GREAT DEAL OF SUCCESS IN THE SPORT, LIKE BEING THE FIRST AMERICAN MALE IN HISTORY TO RECEIVE A PERFECT "10." GYMNASTICS GAVE ME A FEELING OF EXHILARATION THAT HAS BEEN DIFFICULT TO REPLACE. I WORKED AS A STUNT DOUBLE FOR AWHILE, AND ON THE SET OF *BATMAN FOREVER*, AS ROBIN'S DOUBLE, I WAS ALMOST KILLED WHEN AN EXPLOSIVE CHARGE MISFIRED ON THE BATBOAT. *IT WAS AT THAT MOMENT I REALIZED IT WASN'T WORTH THE RISK.* NOW I STICK WITH SAFER, NON-FLAMMABLE ACTING ROLES.

Success has led me on a roller coaster ride. It can sometimes be to your disadvantage to be so well known and have everyone expect so much of you. If you allow yourself to live the image that others have created for you based on your past accomplishments, instead of staying true to the person you are, you can really get lost.

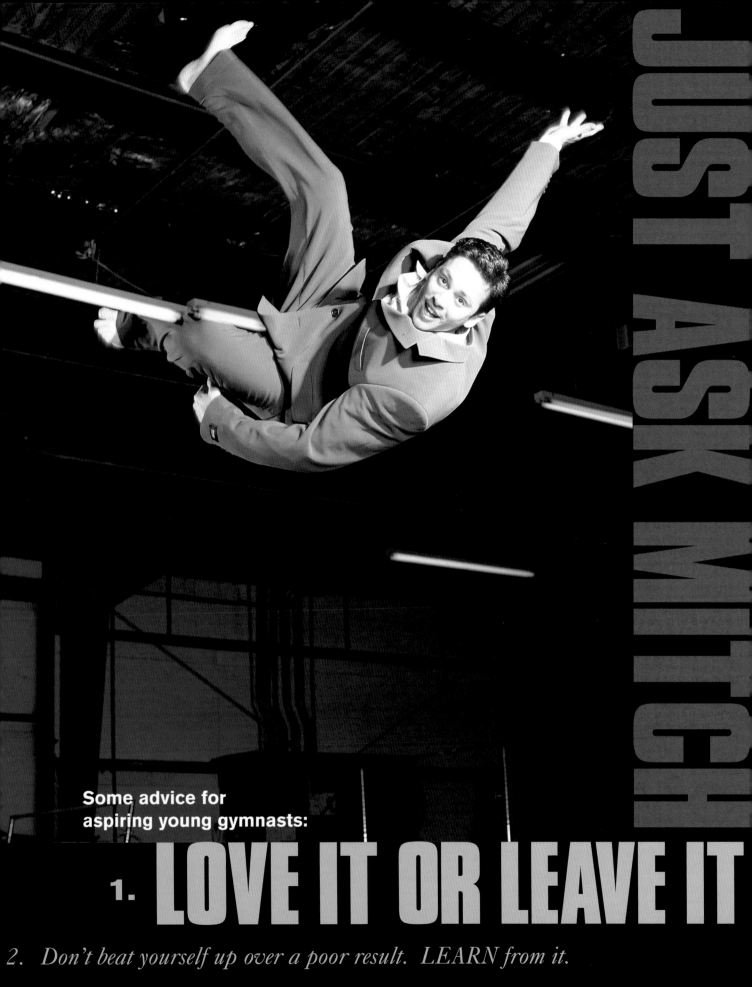

JUST ASK MITCH

Some advice for aspiring young gymnasts:

1. **LOVE IT OR LEAVE IT**

2. *Don't beat yourself up over a poor result.* *LEARN from it.*

3. NEVER let others' opinions determine your greatness.

kerri strug

My first **LOVE** *is gymnastics.*
It gives me
a chance to **EXPRESS** *myself in an ARTISTIC manner.*
The feeling of **FLYING**
is the ultimate **FREEDOM**
of expression.

My short prayer to God gave me the courage and strength to

Strug performed the final

overcome the pain of my injured ankle and perform my second

vault on an injured ankle

vault in Atlanta. I didn't think of it as heroic—I just felt it was my

during the 1996 Olympic

obligation to my teammates and

Games and helped the U.S.

country. I don't consider myself

team clinch the first ever

a celebrity. I'm still

gold medal in the team

starstruck towards the stars

competition.

...to me, I'm just the same old

Kerri.

Kerri Strug and Krasimir Dunev, Santa Monica Pier

BEING IN THE PUBLIC EYE DOESN'T ISOLATE ME FROM THE REAL WORLD. I'M LIKE
EVERY OTHER 19-YEAR-OLD. I GO TO COLLEGE, LIVE IN THE DORMITORY, WAIT IN
LINE AT THE CAFETERIA, AND HANG OUT WITH MY FRIENDS AT THE BEACH.

VITALY
SCHERBO

"I am best of the best…it is so."

—*Vitaly Scherbo*

In Russia, my sad life inspired me. When I was five years old my parents divorced. I lived alone with my mother, and we were very, very poor. Even as a small child I understood that the other children had more than I could ever have. I knew then that I had to change our lives. I also knew that I loved gymnastics and was determined to make that the solution to our problem.

At the Junior National competition, before I became champion, I saw all the top athletes of that time and knew I could be just like them and better if I really wanted to. That's when I made up my mind to become best of the best.

My determination paid off in 1992, when I won six gold medals at the Barcelona Olympics. I won the money and security I needed to take care of my mother. I was young, however, and didn't realize the meaning of athletic accomplishment.

After Barcelona, my life changed. People treated me differently. To become famous is to have people move farther away from you. They become too shy to talk to you and you begin to feel lonely. I try not to let my life be based on my fame — which is ultimately based on someone else's opinions. Their influence on me shouldn't determine who I am as a person. I don't do gymnastics for the fame. I do it because I love it. Of course, there are times when I hate it, like on a bad day when everything is sloppy. But then you take some time off, and when you come back to the gym and execute a big move, you think, "Wow — I really CAN do that!"

"Vitaly Scherbo is the most incredible gymnast I've ever seen. I look at other sports where there's a lot of trash-talking, like basketball and football — a lot of that talk is bogus. Vitaly talks the talk, then goes out and sticks his double double dismount on bars. You've got to applaud him for that."

— Jair Lynch

People say I'm tough—I have to be tough because if I say it is so, then it should be so. I keep my word. I am a perfectionist.

I bring confidence to gymnastics. When I enter a competition I know I won't leave without a medal.

IVAN IVANKOV

When young athletes ask me about gymnastics, I try to teach them what I have learned—to work hard for their goals and to never give up; their luck will come. I want to show them that the sport is all about grace, power, and control—that it should be both refined and explosive at the same time.

Gymnastics is like a casino—a big risk. If you're a good gymnast that's just not enough. You also need luck to be a champion...and few have it. You're either all or nothing. That's the reality.

I snapped my achilles
tendon and missed the
1996 Olympics in Atlanta.
It was as if God said,

**"You're good—
but not good enough—
so try again!"**

The whole experience has
taught me to work even harder to
become better than I am.

FUTURE GOAL:
OLYMPIC GOLD
Nothing will keep me from the next Olympics.
Not INJURY, not MONEY, not TRAINING — NOTHING!

AMANDA BORDEN

9

JAYCIE PHELPS

Amanda is my best friend.

To be a great gymnast, you have to forget about your social life

and focus on your training. You become very

close to the people you train with. When Amanda and I were at the Olympic

Trials, we couldn't imagine only one of us making the team.

We decided we wanted to go to the Olympics *together*, or not at all.

That bond gave us unique strength. When we both made it, we started crying.

We knew that we were on our way together.

— Jaycie

Jaycie and I are like sisters. We've been training

together every day for almost four years, and we've never been competitive with

each other. Friendship is more important. In the gym we're

very serious, and all of our concentration is focused on what we're doing.

It's essential to have someone there for support,

especially when training gets really tough. I would never

have made it through all of the practices and injuries if it

weren't for Jaycie's support.

— Amanda

Being part of a team is absolutely indescribable. I can still envision the arena at the Olympic Games and can hear the crowd of 40,000 chanting, "USA...USA!" It echoed off the walls and surrounded us. That memory gives me the chills. We felt like the whole country was there and was part of our team, cheering us on. When one of us performed a great routine, the excitement and confidence multiplied.

The competition just couldn't catch up. *We were speeding toward victory...*

we were unstoppable

—Jaycie

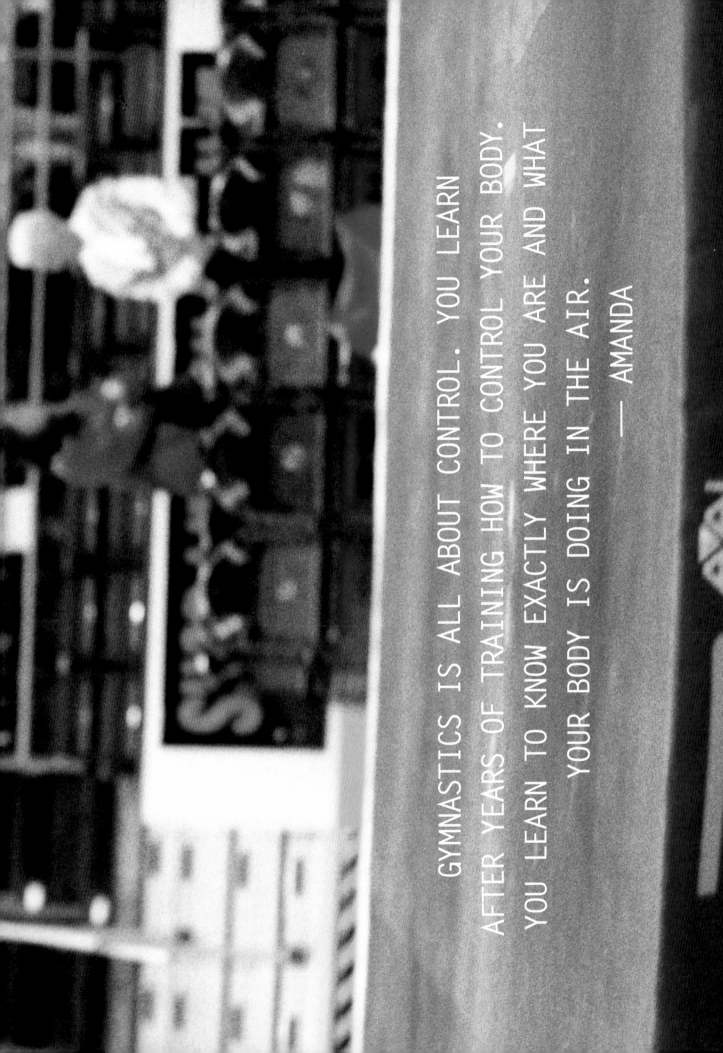

GYMNASTICS IS ALL ABOUT CONTROL. YOU LEARN
AFTER YEARS OF TRAINING HOW TO CONTROL YOUR BODY.
YOU LEARN TO KNOW EXACTLY WHERE YOU ARE AND WHAT
YOUR BODY IS DOING IN THE AIR.

— AMANDA

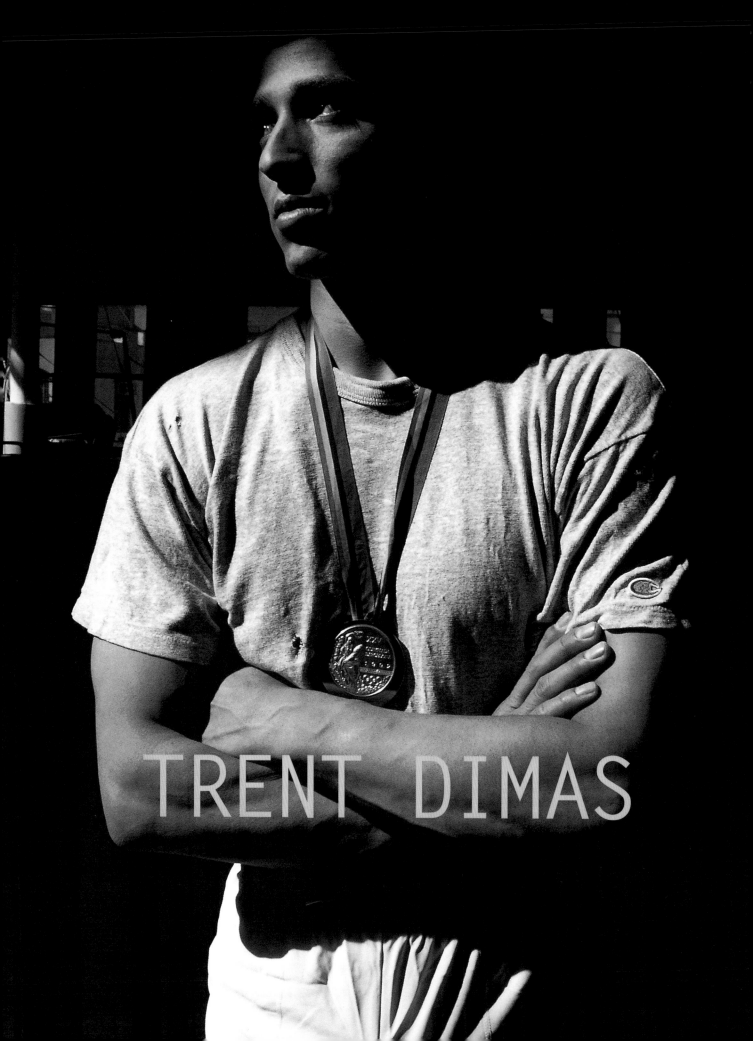

TRENT DIMAS

Do you feel you've attained your goals? As a young child, there were three things I wanted to be: a buffalo, a superhero, and an Olympian. I was able to attain only one of these aspirations, but I think it's the one that fits me best. I spent sixteen years training in Albuquerque, New Mexico, where I grew up. In my family, it is not what we do that is most important, but that we are completely dedicated to whatever we choose. I believe that if I didn't have desire, patience, and integrity, the struggle to be great would have been impossible. To have integrity in life is to be honest with myself and true to my beliefs...not to waver for convenience or money. I have been called difficult at times because of this, but I have never compromised my principles.

Did success come easily? No, I was always the underdog. If there was a team of six men, I was always sixth or even seventh — the guy that just barely made it, or just missed. So when I actually earned a spot on the Olympic team, it was a shock but a dream come true. Even more shocking was when I, the dark horse of the Olympic team, made it all the way to the finals. Then, blowing away everyone's expectations (including my own), I competed like never before and won the gold medal. Not only did I become champion, I was also the only American gymnast to be awarded a medal on foreign soil, as well as the only gymnast to beat a Soviet athlete — Gregory Misutin — in the Olympics. I made it happen when there was no chance of it ever happening. That's the truest success.

Trent Dimas, Sutton Gym, New York

KIM ZMESKAL

My love of gymnastics began at the age of six when I walked into the gym for the first time.

From that point on, it has always been what I want to do. I adored spending up to seven

hours a day at Bela Karolyi's gym. It was my second home. I feel a certain comfort there

like no other place.

My greatest memory of any competition is the 1991 World Championships. The U.S. team won

the silver medal—the highest finish to date. Two days later, I won the all-around title.

It was also Bela's 49th birthday, so it was a great celebration. As a competitive gymnast,

you can't always expect to win. To me, failure only occurs when you don't try your hardest.

I didn't come home from the Barcelona Olympics with a gold medal as everyone predicted, but

I did my best. I wasn't exactly pleased, but it was not a failure.

You have to have dreams and goals. Whether it's to compete at the Level 8 gymnastics meet,

to be an Olympian, or to be a doctor—you have to have something to strive for in life.

Once you find what it is you like, work hard at it and enjoy it. In gymnastics, it's almost

mandatory that you train about 36 hours per week to be competitive. If you're not that committed,

you can't fulfill your potential.

Luckily for retired athletes, gymnastics is now developing a professional afterlife side

of the sport. It's wonderful to be able to continue working in the sport after the competi-

tion ends. How could I really give up something that has given me so much?

I LIKE TO WAKE UP

EVERY DAY KNOWING

THAT THERE IS

A CHALLENGE AHEAD.

ABIE GROSSFELD

INTER
GYMN
CHAM

COLEGI
ASTIC
NSHIP
29

ALL-AROUND
GYMNASTICS CHAMPION
1959

It was a stroke of luck that my first coach at the YMCA was John Van Aaltan, the Olympic hopeful from Holland. Due to the cancellation of the Games during World War II, he ended up in New York. He volunteered his time at the Y because he loved the sport. His European standards are the reason my early training was so excellent.

Another important influence in my developing gymnastics career was my closest friend, Jacques d'Amboise, the ballet dancer. He showed me a lot of the techniques he learned in ballet class, and I used them to add an artistic element to my performance as a gymnast. It was part of what set me apart from the other competitors.

My first competition was in 1953, at the Maccabiah Games in Israel. In those days things were very spartan. The events were held on an outdoor cement basketball court with no mats.

The next time I felt something so powerful was in 1963 when I won the gold medal on the high bar at the Pan American Games. It was my third time, having also won in 1955 and 1959. To me, three times was the charm and at the time it was a record.

I also represented the U.S. for fifteen consecutive years on 26 international teams in 35 countries. I competed in two Olympic Games in 1956 and 1960, and two World Championships.

My transition from competitor to coach was simple. It is so rewarding for me to find kids that have strong ambition and the desire to reach their goals. Especially today, because gymnastics has become so technically difficult that an athlete has to be super dedicated and talented just to begin to try making it. One of the highlights of my more than 34-year career was coaching the men's team at the 1984 Olympic Games to win their first and only team gold medal.

I have seen so many athletes grow to achieve greatness. I saw John Roethlisberger's father train before John was even born. I saw Jair Lynch as a ten year old with budding talent. I saw Mary Lou Retton performing in Japan, a few years before her Olympic achievements. During practice, she performed a double layout and received a standing ovation from the Japanese audience —something that never happens. Although she was small, her power was obvious to me.

Knowing your personal power is the key element to becoming great.

CATHY RIGBY

Moving your body through the difficult skills in gymnastics is a joyous feeling ... but it comes at a price. I'm sure gymnasts feel the same today as I did almost thirty years ago. **The pressures are enormous—always have been...**

I feel my coach, Bud Marquette, and I brought gymnastics to the attention and imagination of Americans at a time when it was virtually an unknown sport. By 1972, every little girl in America knew what gymnastics was. Never before had the sport garnered such attention. We put gymnastics on the map in the USA. When I think about that now, it means more to me than any individual victory.

THERE WAS A TIME WHEN GYMNASTICS WAS MY LIFE. COMPETITION

WAS A MEASURE OF MY WORTH, PERSONALLY AND PROFESSIONALLY.

WHEN I PERFORMED WELL, LIFE WAS GREAT. THANKFULLY,

MY LIFE ISN'T ABOUT WINNING MEDALS ANYMORE.

Gymnastics has opened many doors for me. The sport and its disciplines has given me the confidence to pursue my acting career and has taught me that anything is possible. The two biggest moments in my life were participating in the Olympics and being nominated for a Tony Award for my performance of Peter Pan. Pressure has its rewards.

JOHN ROETHLISBERGER

My father, Fred, and my sister, Marie, were both Olympic gymnasts. My father is now a gymnastics coach at Minnesota State University. It's a great advantage having all that experience on my side. They paved the way for me by getting deeply involved in the sport long before I came along.

In my family, gymnastics is a tradition. I always felt deep inside that I would make it:

I was willing to work hard.

And I was willing to be patient.

As a child, I played other sports, such as soccer and tennis, but gymnastics was never forced upon me. My parents didn't care what activity I chose as long as I put my heart into it and didn't sit at home in front of the television. But in 1984, about the same time my sister made the Olympic team — I was inspired and decided that gymnastics would become my focus.

My father wants the best for me. We have our disagreements, like any father and son, and he is sometimes very hard to please. But I feel it's been the best training experience anyone could have. As a coach, he inspires me to work hard, as a son, I work harder to please him: I have always wanted him to be proud of me. It's a wonderful partnership.

AIR ROET[

WINGSPAN: 84˝

WEIGHT: 150 lbs.

CRUISING ALTITUDE: 25´

MODEL: AMERICAN OLYMPIC

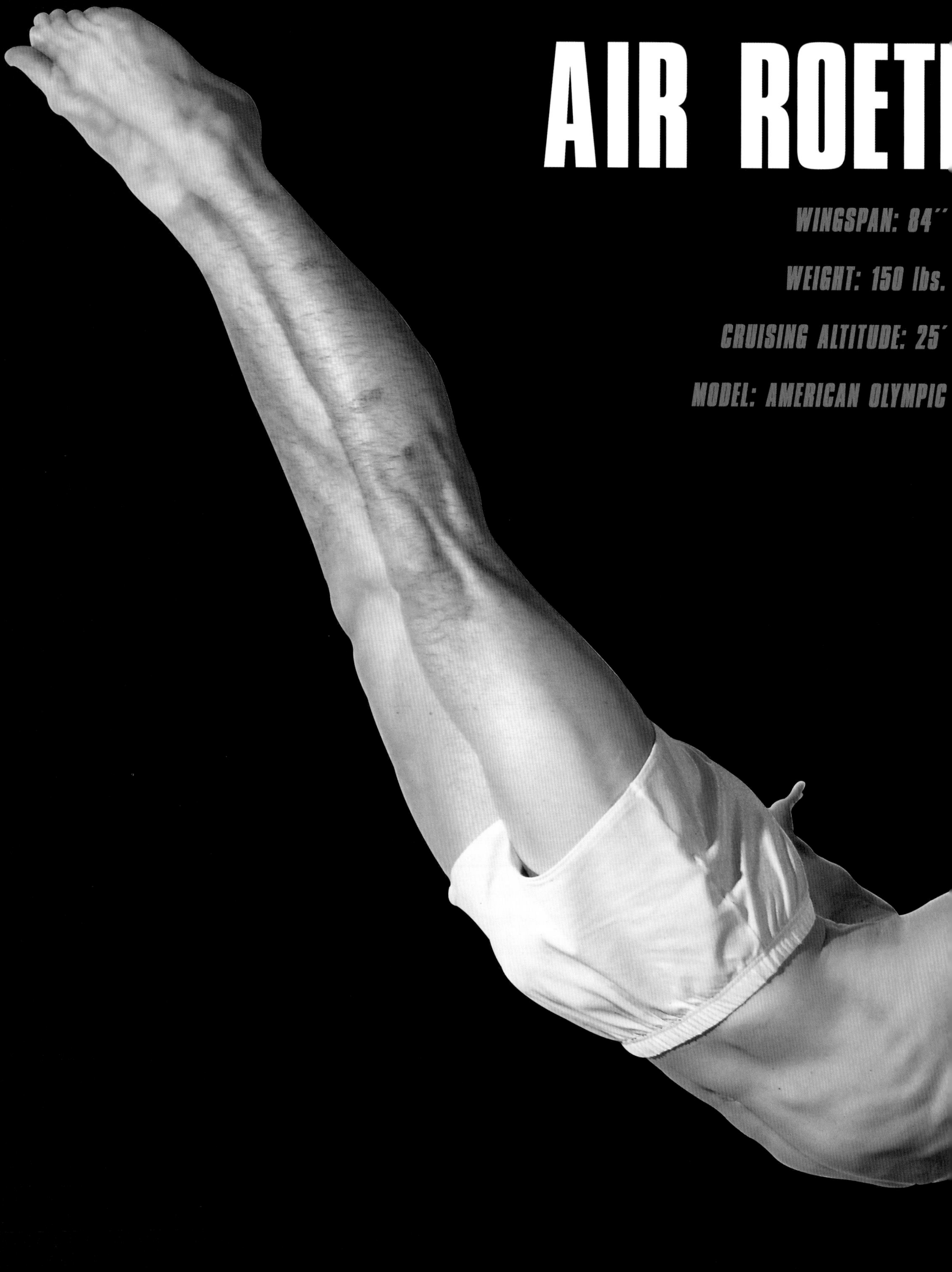

ISBERGER

I'm 26 and have been training in the gym for the past 20 years. I still love learning new tricks — that feeling of flying through the air and scaring myself for the first time. *It's such a rush.* I never get tired of it.

Gymnastics is an extreme sport. *It's one of the sports that you have to train the hardest for—you can't ever get out of shape.* I was recently in Minneapolis with an Olympic decathlete. These guys always talk about having to train really, really hard. A reporter asked him how long before a competition he begins heavy training—his response was, "two months before competition I get serious." I'm standing there thinking, "O.K., the Olympics just ended and I took two weeks off … *if I don't get back to training right now, I'll never be ready for the Games in 2000.*"

The American team went to Argentina for the Pan Am Games in 1994. The crowd there was unruly. As a team we were getting trampled by the Cubans. In the middle of my high bar routine, the crowd started chanting, "fall...fall!" It was my anger that pushed me through and I won the event.

I have *tremendous* pride in my team-mates. We train differently than the Russians or the Chinese...their system supports them so they can train harder and longer. But in the U.S., we have to support ourselves. We go to school, have jobs and other commitments.

By some miracle, we came back in the last event and actually won the competition. They booed us as we stood on the podium and the U.S. national anthem played. I just couldn't believe it—I had never experienced anything like that before.

SVETLANA BOGINSKAYA

At my *very first competition* I placed second. *I was so upset* that the minute I got home, I *threw my medal away. I used to think* gymnastics was only about being *first* and *the best.*

When I started gymnastics class I was very mean to the other girls. I didn't like it when they did better than me so I would make their lives miserable in the locker room so they wouldn't want to come back to the gym. This wasn't good sportsmanship—

but I was just a little girl.

Luckily, I grew up.

I became women's team captain at the 1992 and 1996 Olympics.

My training taught me much more than acrobatics. It taught me compassion, humility, and sportsmanship.

I looked after all the girls, helped them when they were down, and tried to be there when they needed me. I was just as excited for them to do well as I was for myself. I was just like their mother — and I loved it!

I was 15 at my **first** Olympics — too young to realize how important it was. I wasn't even sure I wanted to be there. I almost dropped out two weeks before the Games because I felt tired. My coach nearly had a heart attack. I came home with two gold medals.

I turned 19 just before my **second** Olympics. This time I knew how important the competition was and I felt tremendous pressure. I was also nervous that I was now too old to compete against the younger girls. I just didn't have my usual confidence ... but I brought home a gold medal.

At 23, I found myself at my **third** Olympics. I knew it would be my last one, so I chose to compete simply for the joy of competing. I did it for myself. Even though I didn't win a medal, it was the best competitive experience of my life.

JULIANNE MCNAMARA

GYMNASTICS IS ALL ABOUT

BEING HONEST

WITH YOURSELF

AND BECOMING

STRONGER

THAN YOUR

FEARS.

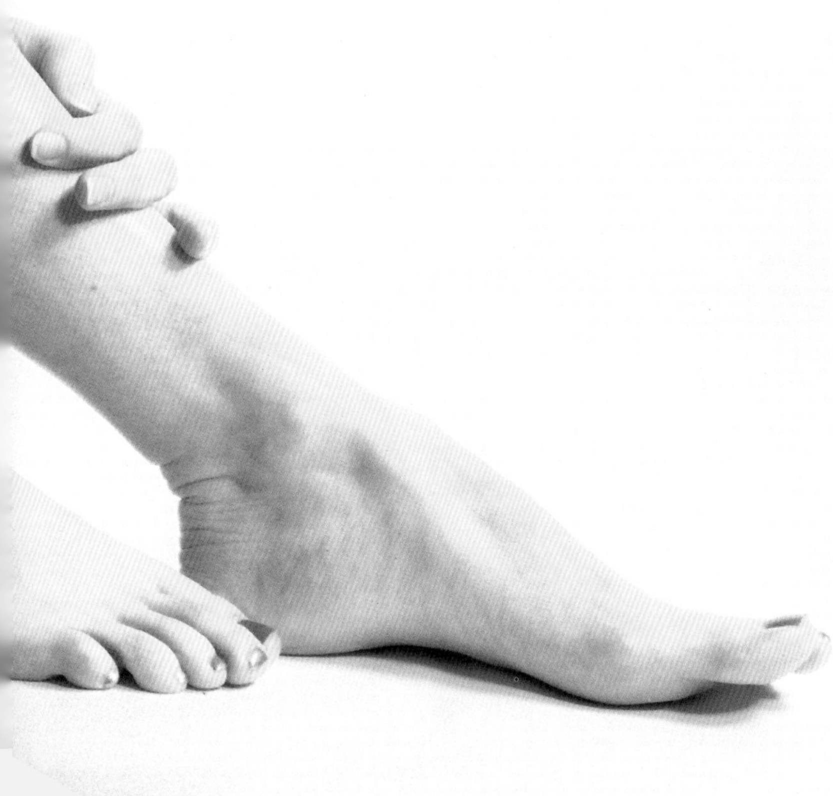

A WORLD-CLASS GYMNAST, LIKE EVERYONE ELSE, HAS SUCCESSES AND FAILURES. *I'VE LEARNED* THROUGH EXPERIENCE THAT THE **QUICKER** YOU LET GO OF FAILURE, AND **LEARN** FROM IT, THE *MORE LIKELY* you are

WHEN YOU DEVELOP THE ABILITY TO SUCCESSFULLY COMPLETE GRAVITY-DEFYING MOVEMENTS WITH YOUR BODY, EVEN THOUGH YOU'RE SCARED TO DEATH, YOUR CONFIDENCE LEVEL SOARS. THE KEY IS KNOWING WHEN TO ACKNOWLEDGE LEGITIMATE FEAR AND TO SET BOUNDARIES.

Gymnastics came naturally to me.
Not that I didn't have to work
hard — but I understood right
away that hard work pays off.
When Bela Karolyi was coaching
me, I immediately accepted the
fact that if I wanted to compete
at the highest level, there
would be no room for complaints
or half-hearted commitment.

TO SUCCEED!

I have lived and loved
gymnastics for over twenty
years. Now that I'm commentating
instead of competing, I have
watched the moves become so much
more extreme. But those simple
rules of achievement I learned
so long ago, still apply today.

muriel
grossfeld

In 1956, I was headed for the Olympics.

When the town paper came to interview me about making the team,

I had to look up "Olympics" in the encyclopedia — it was just a big word to me.

It was different then. In 1953, I didn't even know what a vault was (and neither did most of America). I was a dancer. There was no such thing as a "gym," and my first balance beam routine was practiced on a clothes pole in my mother's living room. I had nowhere to train and no coach to train me. I practiced on a cement floor with no mat. Once a week I was allowed into the men's basketball court with the wooden floor...I taught myself tricks on the balance beam. There was no one to copy so I made up the moves as I went along. My plane was three hours late for my first National Championships in Florida. When I arrived at the door, they called my name to perform a vault. I had never done a vault before— I was still in my street shoes...I imitated the girl ahead of me, and actually got a score. I improvised my entire optional floor routine, and won. I ended up placing fourth on the National Team. My coach couldn't believe it, and said, "Let's go for the Olympics."...My mother was devastated. She wanted me to dance. My father hated it because there was no money involved. Before I started in 1956, there was no music allowed in competitions. I became known for my innovative dance moves. The lack of public awareness was also shocking. Not only did they not know what a balance beam was, when I walked into a gym, they couldn't understand why I didn't look like a six-foot-tall weightlifter. I showed the world that sports were O.K. for women, and that being strong didn't mean being masculine. Most of the time, I was treated like an oddity, sometimes I was treated like a movie star. I made a conscious choice to move away from stardom because I wanted to contribute to others. I knew that eventually I wanted to coach. People would ask me, "Why are you doing this?" I'd say, "What else is there?"

THANK YOU

Bela Karolyi, for his generous efforts

Charles Miers, for this amazing opportunity

Dan Petrucelli, for his endless imagination

Angela Ficks, Aegean Travel, Brooklyn, NYC

Brian, Film & Processing, The Color Resource Center, NYC

Photocare NYC, Photographic Equipment

Joanne and Bill Sotres, Sutton Gym, NYC

Dr. Jon Samuels & Francesca, for all your $upport

Miss Hall's Gym, Houston

Eric Will Gym, La Habra, CA

UCLA Gym, Los Angeles

Mike Rice, Gymcats Gymnastics, Las Vegas

Mr. Ito's Gym, Pensacola, FL

The Bart Conners Gymnastics Academy, Norman, OK

Alice Oldford & Maharajah, Robin's Nest Farm, NJ

All Star Sporting Goods, Times Square, NYC

World Gold Gymnastics Tour

Mr. Paul Ziert, Paul Ziert and Associates, Inc.

Antigravity, NYC

Warner Brothers Studios, Los Angeles

Shannon, Patricia Fields, NYC

Dana Yorio, Hair and Makeup

Fast Eddies Fun Track, Pensacola, FL

Bill Graham Presents, Jefferson Pilot Sports

Mr. Stan Feig

Sheryl Shade, Shade Global, NYC

Wardrobe Stylist: Estee Ochoa

Fashions provided by:
Brooks Brothers
Ceasar Galindo
Elisabetta Rogiani, Los Angeles
Guess?
Hugo Boss
Billy Martins, NYC
Lucille's, NYC
LaCrasia
Rod Keenen
Richard Edwards
North Beach Leather
Matsuda
Levis
Moschino
Patricia Fields, NYC
Paul Smith
Speedo
Yohji Yamamoto

Mom, Maegan's Bay, 1972

This book is dedicated to my parents and parents and caregivers everywhere who encourage children to achieve their dreams. And to my husband, Owen, for his never-ending love and support.

To Lois and David

VIKING
Published by Penguin Group
Penguin Young Readers Group,
345 Hudson Street, New York, New York 10014, U.S.A.
Penguin Group (Canada), 90 Eglinton Avenue East, Suite 700, Toronto,
Ontario, Canada M4P 2Y3 (a division of Pearson Penguin Canada Inc.)

First published in a different form as BUGGY RIDDLES (1986), SNAKEY RIDDLES (1990), and
SPACEY RIDDLES (1992) by Dial Books for Young Readers, a division of Penguin Books USA Inc.

This single-volume edition first published in 2008 by Viking, a division of Penguin Young Readers Group

10 9 8 7 6 5 4 3 2 1

ISBN 978-0-670-01121-6
LC number: 2008015550

Manufactured in China

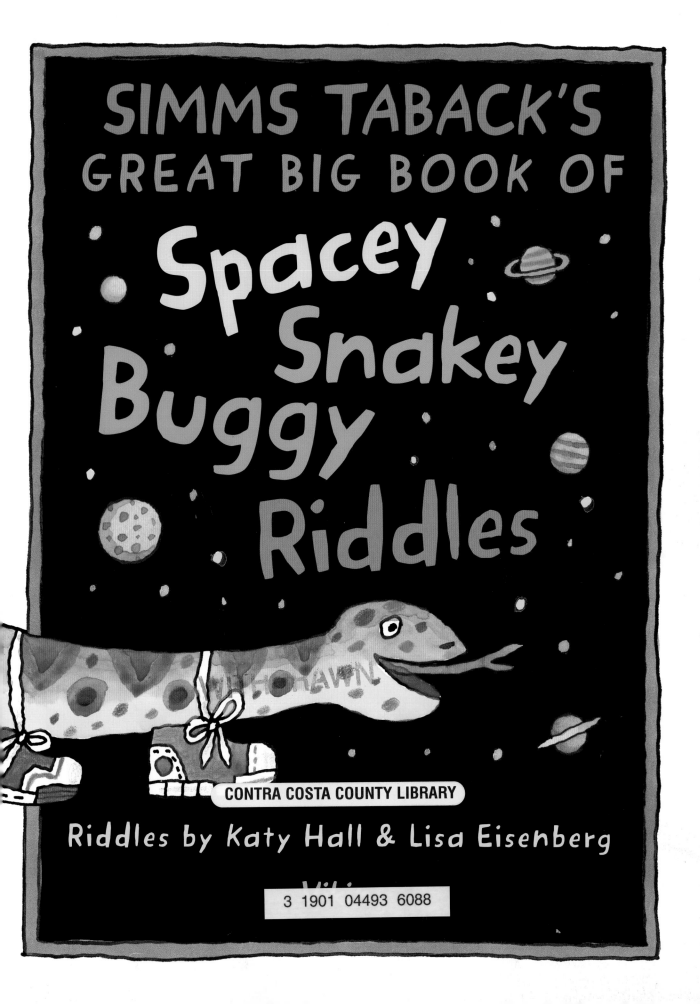

SIMMS TABACK'S
GREAT BIG BOOK OF
Spacey
Snakey
Buggy
Riddles

Riddles by Katy Hall & Lisa Eisenberg

Viking

Everyone has a favorite riddle. This is mine.

Why couldn't the little snake count up to ten?

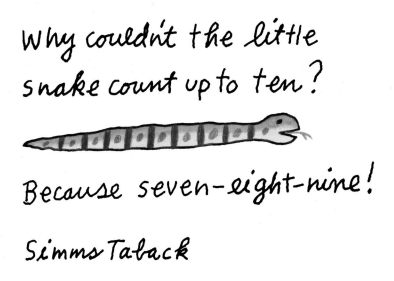

Because seven-eight-nine!

Simms Taback

What do you call two spiders who just got married?

Newly webs!

What does a polite snake
say after he bites you?

"Fangs a lot!"

On what day do spiders
eat the most?

Flyday!

What's big and bright and silly?

A fool moon!

What do you call a crazy spaceman?

An astro-nut!

What kind of shoes do reptiles wear?

Snakers!

What kind of songs
do planets like to sing?

Nep-tunes!

Did you hear about the two snakes
who met in the revolving door?

They started going around together!

What kind of jacket
would you wear on the sun?

A blazer!

Where should a 300-pound
space alien go?

On a diet!

What do you say when
you tickle a baby mosquito?

"Itchy-kitchy-koo!"

How do you keep a mosquito from biting you on Monday?

Swat it on Sunday!

What do you have to know
to teach a snake tricks?

More than the snake!

What's soft and white and comes from Mars?

A Mars-mallow!

What do you get when you cross
a caterpillar and a bee?

A fuzzy yellow jacket!

What did the snake say
when she stopped biting the giraffe's neck?

"It's been nice gnawing you!"

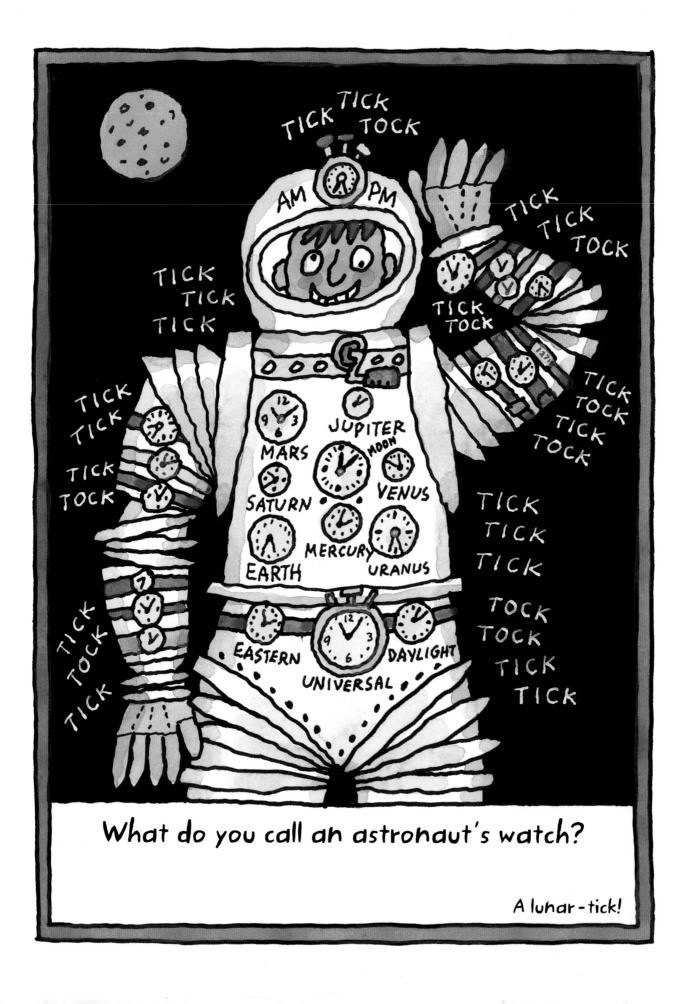

What do you call an astronaut's watch?

A lunar-tick!

What did the moon say to the star?

Boy, are you far out!

How many family members came to the picnic?

Three sisters, two uncles, and 10,000 ants!

What did the mosquito say
when she got a stomachache?

It must have been someone I ate!

Why is a cloud like Santa Claus?

Because it holds the rain, dear!

If dogs have fleas,
what do sheep have?

Fleece!

Where do flies go to dance?

To the fly ball!

What did the cobra say
to the flute player?

Charmed to meet you!

What's the best way to talk to a Martian?

Long distance!

How did the astronauts
lock the spaceship door?

With a lightning bolt!

What do you get if you cross two bees
with a water pistol?

A bee-bee gun!

What do snakes put on their kitchen floors?

Reptiles!

What do spiders like
with their hamburgers?

French flies!

Why is the North Star the smartest star?

Because it's the brightest!

Why didn't the owl eat the green snake?

He was waiting for it to ripen!

Which is heavier,
a half moon or a full moon?

A half moon, because a full moon is lighter!

What poem can you find in outer space?

A uni-verse!

What do you get if you cross
a centipede and a parrot?

A walkie-talkie!

What do bugs have
that no other animal has?

Baby buggies!

Why did the neighbors get tired
of the anaconda's music?

Because all he could play were his scales!

Why shouldn't you grab a snake's tail?

It's only his tail,
but it could be your end!